W9-AYQ-922

FEVER

ELAINE LANDAU

 Marshall Cavendish
Benchmark
New York

Marshall Cavendish Benchmark
99 White Plains Road
Tarrytown, New York 10591
www.marshallcavendish.us

Expert Reader: Leslie L. Barton, MD, Professor Emerita of Pediatrics,
University of Arizona College of Medicine, Tucson, Arizona

Library of Congress Cataloging-in-Publication Data

Landau, Elaine.
Fever / by Elaine Landau.
p. cm. — (Head-to-toe health)
Includes bibliographical references and index.
Summary: "Provides basic information about fever and how to care for yourself with one"—Provided by publisher.
   ISBN 978-0-7614-3499-3
   1. Fever—Juvenile literature. I. Title.
   RB129.L38 2010
   616.047—dc22
   2008022987

Editor: Christine Florie
Publisher: Michelle Bisson
Art Director: Anahid Hamparian
Series Designer: Alex Ferrari

Photo research by Candlepants Incorporated

Cover Photo: Peter Dazeley / Getty Images

The photographs in this book are used by permission and through the courtesy of:
Getty Images: AFP, 4; Gunnar Kullenberg, The Stock Connection, 10; Dr. David Phillips, 12; Victoria Blackie, 26; Peter Dazeley. Minden Pictures: David Tipling, 6. Photo Researchers Inc.: David R. Frazier, 7. Corbis: Heide Benser, zefa, 15; Jose Luis Pelaez, Inc., 23. Alamy Images: PhotoAlto, 16; Purestock, 24. Photo Edit Inc.: Bill Aron, 19. Shutterstock, 20.

Printed in Malaysia
1 3 5 6 4 2

CONTENTS

YOUR BODY TEMPERATURE

What if you were an alligator instead of a kid? Your skin would be scaly rather than smooth. You'd also have a long, strong tail and lots more teeth than you have now. Besides these differences, you'd be a cold-blooded animal. In this case, cold-blooded doesn't mean cruel or unfeeling. The term describes an animal whose body temperature changes with its surroundings.

When an alligator is cold, it will rest in the sun. Before long, that alligator will warm up. What if an alligator gets too hot? Then it finds a cool, shady spot where it can cool off, or it can always go for a swim.

Things work very differently for people. Unlike alligators, crocodiles, snakes, fish, and other cold-blooded animals, humans are warm-blooded. That means their body temperature

◄ Even if you are playing outside on a cold day, your body temperature remains the same.

COOLING OFF

Other creatures in the animal world are warm-blooded like humans. They sweat to cool off, too. Monkeys and apes have sweat glands all over their bodies. Dogs, however, have sweat glands only on their feet. So how do they cool off? Have you ever seen a dog pant when it's hot? Like sweating, panting is a way for its body to lose heat. Some warm-blooded animals also cool off by going for a swim. Whales and dolphins are warm-blooded animals without any sweat glands. Yet they don't overheat because they keep cool in the water.

usually stays the same—is stable. It does not change with their surroundings.

So what happens when you're playing outdoors on a really hot day? Your body sends a message to your brain. It lets your brain know that your body is heating up.

Your brain, in turn, sends back a signal to your body. It tells your body to sweat. This cools your skin and your body loses heat. As a result, you don't overheat.

When your body heats up, signals are sent to your brain telling your body to sweat. Sweating is your body's air conditioning system.

If you're outside when it's cold, the opposite happens. Your body feels the lower temperature. A message goes to the brain and back, letting you know that it's time to do something about it—to put on some warmer clothes or to go inside and warm up with a cup of hot cocoa.

YOUR NORMAL BODY TEMPERATURE

Most humans have a body temperature of about 98.6 degrees Fahrenheit (37 °Celsius). Some people's normal temperature can be a bit lower. Other people have a normal body temperature that's a little higher. Yet it remains around 98.6 °F.

At times, however, your temperature may shoot up. One day you might wake up not feeling very well. You might feel achy and uncomfortable and your temperature might be 102 °F (38.9 °C) or higher. Your body is not behaving as it usually does. What's happening to you? You're sick and you've got a fever!

SOMETHING'S NOT RIGHT

All kinds of signs surround us. Some signs tell us what things are. Other signs help keep us safe. A stop sign tells cars to stop. This can keep an accident from happening.

Fever is a different kind of sign. In a way, it's a warning sign. If you have a fever, you know that something's not right inside your body.

WHAT'S GOING ON?

You've probably had fevers in the past when you were sick. But did you know why? To find out more about fever, we'll need to take a closer look at the brain.

THE BRAIN GAME

The **hypothalamus** is the part of the brain that rules when it comes to temperature. Just as a **thermostat** controls the temperature of a room, the hypothalamus controls your body's temperature. Think of it as your body's thermostat. When you are well, your body's thermostat, or hypothalamus, keeps your temperature at about 98.6 °F (37 °C).

But what happens when germs invade your body? Then your body defends itself. It has its own army of germ fighters ready to do this.

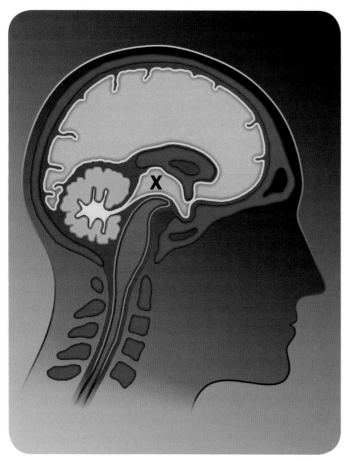

The hypothalamus (X above) is a part of the brain that controls the temperature of the body.

HOW MUCH DO YOU KNOW ABOUT YOUR TEMPERATURE?

See if you can answer the True or False question below:

Question: When you are well, your temperature doesn't change.

The right answer is false. Are you surprised? Even when you aren't sick, your temperature changes a little throughout the day.

Your body temperature is lowest in the early morning—from about 1:00 AM to 7:00 AM. It's a little higher in the late afternoon and early evening—from about 4:00 PM to 9:00 PM.

Your body temperature can also rise a degree or two after eating or exercising. Very hot weather, an overheated room, or bundling up in too much warm clothing can have the same effect.

LET THE BATTLE BEGIN!

Fever is one of your body's defenders, or germ fighters. The hypothalamus calls it to action. Instead of having your temperature remain about 98.6 °F (37 °C), it shoots up higher.

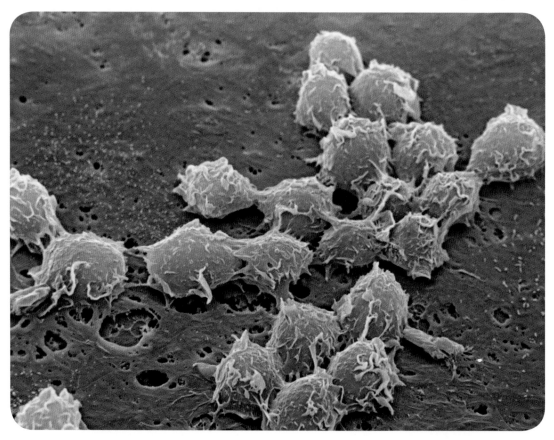

White blood cells, seen here through a high-powered microscope, fight off viruses in the body.

Your body turns up the heat for a reason. Scientists think that germs don't like heat. When you have a fever, your body gets very warm. That makes it a less comfortable place for germs to live and multiply.

The fever helps your body in other ways, too. It alerts your body to make more white cells. White cells are champion germ fighters.

YOU MEAN FEVER'S A GOOD THING?

Having a fever is really helpful. Without it, people might not always know that something is wrong. They might not do what they need to do to get well. That might mean not going to a doctor or taking some medicine they need.

Bet you never thought of fever as your friend. Yet it plays an important role in keeping you well.

Having a Fever

Here's a quick quiz for you.

Which of these things happen when you have a fever?

A. Your toenails stop growing for at least two weeks.

B. There may be a temporary change in your eye color.

C. You may feel quite chilly and even shiver.

Answers *A* and *B* are wrong. Fever will not stop your toenails from growing. It won't change your eye color either.

The right answer is *C*. Yet does that sound right? After all, doesn't a fever make you feel hot—not cold?

SO WHAT'S THE STORY?

Chills often occur once your body's thermostat sets your temperature higher. That's because shivering is a way that the body produces heat. So while you're getting hot, you might feel quite cold. The chills will stop once your temperature reaches its new higher level.

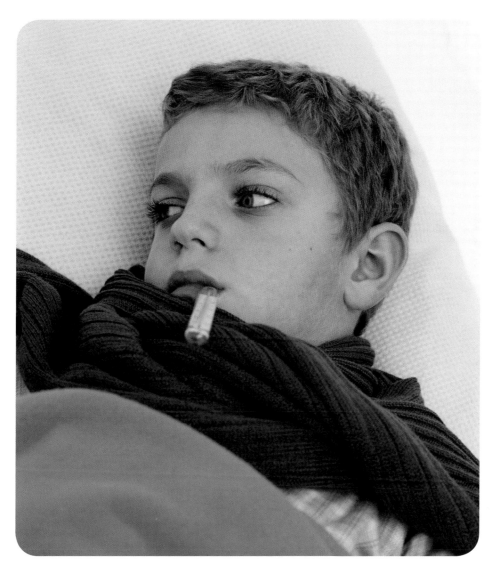

When you have a fever you may get chills. Shivering makes heat which fights off germs.

Fever will make you feel achy, weak, and sleepy.

HOW LONG WILL YOU HAVE A FEVER?

Usually a fever lasts for only a few days. Yet how long a fever lasts will vary. That's because fever in itself is not an illness. It's a symptom, or sign, of an illness. A sore throat or a cough are symptoms, too.

Depending on what's making you sick, other symptoms may occur when you have a fever. These often include feeling weak, achy, and sleepy. You may also have a headache and not feel like eating.

Once the illness goes away, your higher body temperature will go down. At that point your body needs to get rid of the extra heat caused by the fever. It does this by sweating. You won't want your heavy blanket or a hot water bottle now! You'll be feeling warm and damp as you sweat.

DID YOU KNOW?

Sometimes people get fevers that aren't due to an illness. A bad sunburn can trigger a fever. At times, fever can be a side effect of some medicines. Kids may also have a fever after getting the **vaccinations** they need for school. Other things can cause fevers as well.

Yuck! You're Sick

Fever is most often caused by an illness, or **infection** in your body. There are lots of infections that cause fever. One infection that kids often get is strep throat.

Strep throat is caused by small **bacteria** invaders. When you have strep throat, your throat feels very sore and hurts when you swallow. You may also have a headache and fever.

Doctors give **antibiotics** for strep throat. Such drugs kill the strep bacteria. After taking this medicine, you'll soon feel much better.

OUCH, MY EAR HURTS

Lots of kids also get earaches or ear infections. When you have one, your ear can really hurt. You may have a fever, too. Your ear has three parts. Your outer ear is the part you see. Inside are your middle and inner ear. Ear infections happen

Ear infections can cause fever.

TAKING YOUR TEMPERATURE

Think you may have a fever? There's only one way to know for sure. Have your temperature taken. Always wait a half hour after eating or drinking to have your temperature taken orally (in your mouth). Also take any gum or candy out of your mouth. You don't want anything to affect the right reading of your temperature.

The thermometer should be put under your tongue. Close your lips around it to hold it in place. Breathe through your nose, and do not bite down on the thermometer. Before you know it, you'll have a reading. Now you'll know for sure if you have a fever.

when germs invade your middle ear. Your body springs into action to fight those germs. Soon that part of your ear becomes filled with a yellowish white fluid called **pus**.

Pus contains the white cells your body produces to fight the infection and the germs killed in the attack. As the pus builds up, the pressure on your ear hurts. The pain of an earache plus having a fever can make you feel pretty miserable.

If your doctor thinks bacteria are to blame here, you may be given an antibiotic. Then the problem often clears up in a few days.

OH, NO! IT'S THE FLU

Still another infection that causes fever is the flu. The flu can give you a cough and headache, too. You may feel tired and achy as well.

The flu is caused by a **virus**. Viruses are extremely tiny germs. They are even too small to see without a special microscope.

When you have the flu, you need lots of rest. You should also drink plenty of fluids. You'll usually feel better in a week or two.

These are just a few of the infections that often cause fever. There are many others as well. Yet in each case, fever is one of the symptoms that lets you know there's a problem.

TREATING A FEVER

Let's face it, fever may be helpful, but having one is just no fun. There are some things you can do to feel better, though. Keep reading to find out what they are.

REST IS BEST

Try to get lots of rest when you have a fever. Running around or playing hard is not a good idea now. Sometimes such activity can cause your body heat to rise even higher.

Pass the time doing quiet things. Read a book, draw, or watch TV. You can play soccer and run races once you're better.

HOW ABOUT A BATH?

Sometimes, taking a bath when you have a fever is helpful. It can lower your temperature and make you feel less achy. The bath water should be **tepid**. That means not too hot or too cold— just lukewarm.

One of the best ways to treat a fever is to get a lot of rest and do quiet activities.

RAH, RAH WATER!

Drink lots of water when you have a fever. Sweating is part of your body's natural cooling system. That means you use up a lot of fluids when your temperature rises.

To replace fluids that are lost during fever, be sure to drink plenty of liquids.

You don't have to drink only water to replace your fluids. Juice, sports drinks, and soup are good as well. Having a dish of Jell-O or your favorite flavored ice pop will also do the trick. After all, your body is made up of 60 percent water—so don't skimp on the fluids.

MEDICINE FOR A FEVER? MAYBE.

If your fever isn't very high, 102 °F (38.9 °C) or below, often no medicine will be given for it. Your doctor, however, may give you medicine for the infection causing the fever. When the infection goes away, so does the fever.

At times, medicine may also be given to lower a very high fever that is making you uncomfortable. One of the medicines most commonly given for this is **acetaminophen**, sold as Tylenol, Tempra, Anacin-3, or Datril. Another medicine used to lower temperature is **ibuprofen**. Common brand names for this medicine are Advil or Motrin.

These medicines do not cure the infection causing the fever. They work by helping to lower the body's heat. Children and young teens should never be given aspirin for fever. It can lead to a very serious illness known as Reye's syndrome.

STAY HEALTHY

The best way to avoid a fever is not to get sick. There are things you can do to stay healthy and fit. Eating a healthy diet is a great first step in the right direction. Be sure to get the right amount of both exercise and rest as well. Also, always wash your hands after using the bathroom and before eating. This helps stop the spread of germs.

Of course, you might still get sick and have a fever. Just remember that fevers don't last forever. Before long, you'll be well and feeling as good as new!

One way to avoid getting sick is by eating healthy foods.

GLOSSARY

acetaminophen — (also known as Tylenol, Tempra, Anacin-3, or Datril) a medicine used to lower fever

antibiotic — a drug that kills certain types of germs

bacteria — small germs that multiply in the body

hypothalamus — the part of the brain that controls your temperature

ibuprofen — (also known as Advil or Motrin) a medicine used to lower fever

infection — a condition caused by the invasion and growth of germs in the body

pus — a yellowish white fluid that contains the white cells your body produces to fight infection and the debris of germs killed

tepid — something that is lukewarm

thermostat — a device that controls temperature in a home heating system

vaccinations — substances that protect you from getting various illnesses

virus — very tiny germs that can be seen only with a special microscope

FIND OUT MORE

BOOKS

Glaser, Jason. *Flu*. Mankato, MN: Capstone Press, 2006.

————. *Strep Throat*. Mankato, MN: Capstone, 2007.

Mitchell, Melanie. *Killing Germs*. Minneapolis, MN: Lerner Books, 2006.

Royston, Angela. *Staying Healthy*. Chicago: Raintree, 2004.

Sherman, Josepha. *The War Against Germs*. New York: Rosen Publishing Group, 2004.

Verdick, Elizabeth. *Germs Are Not For Sharing*. Minneapolis, MN: Free Spirit, 2005.

Weber, Rebecca. *Healthy Habits*. Minneapolis, MN: Compass Point Books, 2004.

DVDS

Drugs & Disease. Schlessinger Media, 2005.

Personal Health & Hygiene (Health for Children). Schlessinger Media, 2005.

WEB SITES

A Kid's Guide to Fever

www.kidshealth.ort/kid/ill_injure/sick/fever.html

This Web site is a great guide to what fever is and what to do when you have one.

Lather Up For Good Health

www.colgate.com/app/LatherUpForGoodHealth/US/Kids.cvsp

Visit this Web site for some special activities that can make hand washing fun.

INDEX

Page numbers in **boldface** are illustrations.

About the Author

Award-winning author Elaine Landau has written more than three hundred books for young readers. Many of these are on health and science topics. For Marshall Cavendish, she has written *Asthma*; *Bites and Stings*; *Broken Bones*; *Bumps, Bruises, and Scrapes*; *Cavities and Toothaches*; and *The Common Cold* for the Head-to-Toe Health series.

Landau received a bachelor's degree in English and journalism from New York University and a master's degree in library and information science from Pratt Institute. You can visit Elaine Landau at her Web site: www.elainelandau.com.

FEB   2011